Sunset Strands

POEMS

Satyapal Anand

Order this book online at www.trafford.com
or email orders@trafford.com

Most Trafford titles are also available at major online book retailers.

Printed in the United States of America.

ISBN: 978-1-4669-0728-7 (sc)
ISBN: 978-1-4669-0727-0 (hc)
ISBN: 978-1-4669-0726-3 (e)

Library of Congress Control Number: 2011962222

Trafford rev. 12/13/2011

   www.trafford.com

North America & international
toll-free: 1 888 232 4444 (USA & Canada)
phone: 250 383 6864 ♦ fax: 812 355 4082

CONTENTS

FOR

DAISY & SACHIN

In a Station of the Metro
(Ezra Pound wrote a poem with this title – 1911)

"The apparition of those faces in the crowd
Petals on a wet black bough."

O Ezra, it is a century since your time
Your alter-ego Satyapal is in a metro station
In Washington D.C., the famed flower town of America.
Wet indeed are the pavements;
Black bows of trees are bent with
Car-exhaust blackened melting snow.
Unlike London of a century back
Where you didn't see black faces
The apparitions here are almost all black
Negro, no, black, nada; African-American, yes,
White ghosts here don't ride the metro
They cruise by in silver cars;
Company-owned limousines
Liveried chauffeurs drive the worthies
To and fro their centrally heated offices.

Ezra, had you been your namesake
A mere twenty-five centuries ago
A scribe, prophet and reformer
Helping the Hebrew nation in ways divers
You might have, in London of a century since,
Done the same for your own nation
Ruled by red-neck roosters of the Empire
On which the sun never set.
For the war that was not yet christened
The World War One was looming large
On the horizon, if any horizon the empire had.

Ezra, unlike your alter-ago here today
You never felt the pain of the subject nations
Like India with untold wealth of yore
Where loin-clothed men lived on ten pence a day
Or South Africa of Apartheid's shameless fame.

Ezra, you had much else to do.
Busy you were yourself with melting metaphors
Sibilant similes and words warbling on poetic numbers
No time, no, nothing – you had no inkling
Of what was happening in India or Africa.
Your ink was spent in worming word pictures
Homologous homilies in image clusters
Satisfied you were with what you did.

Your alter-ego that I am, Ezra,
I am a disaffected self, for I was born in India
The brightest gem in the British crown.
My ancestors served Queens and Kings,
Victorias, Edwards and Georges.

A poet nonetheless I am
And I see the black apparitions in a metro station
As people, exploited, imposed upon and drained
By the progeny of the same European masters
Your sons and their sons and their sons
Those who live in America today;
And in my poems I present them
'Petals at a wet black bough'
In their true black hues.
So, forgive me, if you can
But forgive yourself, you mustn't.

∗

The Short Hand of Emotion

"Music is the shorthand of emotion."—Leo Tolstoy.

A debauch of sounds, said I,
But worthy of notice if harmony is restored
Organs and instruments play as friends;
Not as enemies out to cut each others' throats.

True, she said, but do remember
Music is composed before it is played
Written in a funny language it is.
What Mozart said, badly written, would give
a rancid smell if not a bad taste.
I write my music as a sow piddles, he had said.
A sow is a filthy animal—and its piddling?
Does it ring a sound sweet enough for music?

No, I said, but a sound is a sound.
If produced in a symphonic harmony, it's music.
You don't see a sow piddling with your mind's eye.
You use your ears, better still if the eyes are shut.

Ears, ears! She said rather unmusically
Instruments used sheep's entrails for strings, you know
Not for nothing that Shakespeare said
In *Much Ado About Nothing*: Is it not strange
That sheep's guts should hale souls out of men's bodies?
If Addison calls it 'All of heaven we have below'
Then sheep's guts and a sow's piddling are our heaven.

The bard contradicted himself so often
One wonders why he wasn't knighted.
He talks about sheep's guts in one breath

And then in *Twelfth Night* calls it the food of love
Give me excess of it; he says, that surfeiting,
The appetite may sicken, and so die.

Pooh! Says my lady love, didn't you read Caruso,
Enrico Caruso, you know who said that what you do
When you shit, singing is the same thing, only up.
If music is a shitty or a piddling business
I've nothing else to say, my dear.

Beauty and Geometry

Euclid, it was, who had looked at beauty bare
Says 'Edna St. Vincent Millay
She a beauty though undressed only in her poems.'
How's it the men have always sung praises
Of beauty—unsung by women, be they poetesses.
Three centuries before the savior
Who never uttered a word about female beauty
This geo-metric measure-happy Greek
Sized up spread and bounds and borders
Surfaces and solids – their length or tilt
Angles and magnitudes – their properties and relations
On paper with a pencil or a pen.

Beauty's skin-deep says one, and goes on to say
Momentary though in mind, in the flesh
It becomes immortal; no truth in this, says another,
For beauty is not everlasting, dust is.

Ask a toad what is beauty
The answer if the toad, could it speak in human voice
Would simply be: a female with two round eyes
A large flat mouth, a yellow belly and a brown back.
So there you are, my man, singing of beauty
Sublime and solemn, ethereal and inspiring.
Be a toad or a Euclid
But never a Keats to know what is beauty.
Shall that be the epitaph of this poem?

The Great Mother Goddess I See

I have no mystic threads woven through me
That to design my fabric weaves.
No golden strand streams from my lips
Adorning the stalk of the goddess sheaves
No blue tranquility adds my heart
To one last expanse of her moon-framed robe.
Nor pink remorse of my shame stains
The bowl beneath her right heel broke.

Alpha and Omega, says the Bible
Beginning and the end, the first and the last
God thus speaks in first person
But if God's gender is what we know it is
He would be issueless unless there is a mother.
So do I worship the life-giver mother-goddess?

Resplendent, by her lover-sons rose
Who laurel chew in amorous groves
While on the burning ground the heart
Of fiery demons she grinning holds
In creative impregnation.

With moon and stars for brow and toes
And tears of rains and flashing hands,
Doubly the hails and halos grow
By secret and sacred elevation.
And while her wondering subjects watch
Virtuously she bears
Fruit of a holy consummation.

Midsummer Madness

Day-night blazing drenching
Burning, dark-warm dew
Sun-star time enchanting
Casts a spell
Upon passions in nature and man.

The unrestrained love commands
The day is followed by the night out.
Springing fresh-eyed in the dawn,
Busy in the heat of morning.
Voluptuous in the shadowed afternoon
Hushing talk to wonder in the love-laced twilight
And changing wonder for delight.

The same unrestrained love commands
The man in the house, young and virile
To follow his mate up the stairs
Down into the kitchen
Further down into the basement.
Dinner talk, pre-nuptial play
The drama itself, played from first
To the last act is the rain of man's seed
Till curtains are drawn
And the night thickens.

In the garden a drama plays itself out
In the moon-burned, star-stung night
The drunken flowers reel around
And in a mist of golden pollen
Toss their delicate semen down.

Dandelions Spring

Winter over,
Greenness floods the land
From tree-sky height to ground.
Sap moves beneath the crust of hoary trees
And tender leaves burst out on gnarly boughs.

The human kingdom feels
The spring air and its limbs wake up
To the clarion call of the generative season.
Overcoats are thrown away, sweaters abandoned
Woolies discarded for another year.
Fresh, fulsome, rosy and blooming
Human bodies are bared
Partly at least. Bright and glowing
Wholesomely rounded are breasts
Bobbing with beauteous bounce.

Out from her silken shelter in the garden
Comes a wrinkled butterfly
Rubbing the season's sleep
From her drowsy pop-eyes.
A shocked relief it is that she finds
In her new form, a flower floating in the air.

Below the tree through the timid grass
Dandelions poke their rough-mane heads
And softly grow.

The Race Track

(George Islington wrote a poem with this title – 1980)

I held her reins archly
Slapped her neck smartly
Calling her Red for her painted red mane.
Same as my hair as it sang red-red-rock
She rode without holding her bridle
Or even the pole for her balancing act.
As if she's feeling
The wild beast springing between her legs.

How best she could control him
By the force of a leg-squeeze alone.
I admired her dexterity.

Rising and dripping of salty sweat
Drop by drop, drip, drip, drip
To the churn of merry-go-round
The horse became wooden;
Sprinting and scampering and kicking
(Something indeed quite thrilling)
The high note once trilling
Sagged chillingly chilling,
Flooded the spring of her swollen hair
She shrank from the tiger's eye
Glass-eyed grinning
Unmanned by her lover-trainer.

Painted, paper, dream – adjectives galore
Pine, tiger, jungle – nouns also matched
Wooden horse, rubber pole, brass breathing
Up and down, up and down
Turning nowhere round and round
To the knowing smirk of the creaky bed.

A Whore in China
(Allen Ginsberg wrote a poem with this title – 1960)

Chalk-faced with stiffly patterned rolls
Of formal hair, a black and white design.
Face—reminiscent of Genghis, Tao and Buddha
Of centuries slumbered, unnumbered.
Eyes . . . they flat? Slanted? Skewed?
None, yet sporty, smart and spruce.
Lips . . . they cushioned? Padded and buffered?
Yes, but creases under crimson paint
Call a halt to a close caution.
Painted, bow mouth – sullen?
No, elegantly withdrawn within
Smile-soft, smirk-slithered
Elegantly inviting
To be star-studded by an American.

Is still, is
Negligent
Hesitant, carefully crafted
In open solicitation
Glancing sideways at a cop
A Thai lad with an Indian lass
Sari, sarong, sumptuous tummy-tickling laughter
A shrieking she-mammoth
And a neighing he-horse.

"Shall come? Good sex, good wine, good bed.
Shall come? You? Handsome American!"

Sex in the art
And the lady artist
With the gentleman easel
Both – their own artifacts.

Back in the Village

(Ann Baudelaire wrote a poem with this title – 1907)

The grasshoppers are singing, and from
Your feet, songs to Olympus bringing.
Swill deep, old soak, of your sap they're wringing
You—of—a-classroom-black-board-bard
Dry of your ferment
Blind, old and bald
A single eyeglass tucked to the nose-tip
Come to the village a-singing
Of your childhood, eh?

Dreamt you ever
Of the man hanged upside down?
Before he was strung up the wrong way around?
Could you have said no – none – nada
Latino tongued?
Couldn't have said it, you know.

See, here comes (Oh, but you can't see!)
Here comes the hopper to hop up
On your toe, or whatever it is, a stub at the best.
I am mad enough for more, you muse
And full of gusto, before I die
You daydream and ruminate
But who is there to listen to you?

What do you say of dying?
Hair sprouting in the ground –
Can you see from your roots?
Oh, you can say now
I was double-dared and dying of excess.
Excess of what?

Of blackboard-and-classroom-castrations?
Coffee House carousals?
Library lubrications with eye-drops?
O professor, be careful of what they call
Moral turpitude.

Unstrung done (the hopper's gone a-jumping)
To wait in the bushes for another spree
And you of the new-rooted
Are blowing a now muted
Burden thru this dim-lighted rough lane
From the life-careless with a ho-hum-hewing,
Mind it—all the old, unspent, useless are dying.

Teaching ? No more
Blackboard ? No more
Classroom castrations? No more
Coffee House carousals? No more
Library lubrications? No, more, Sir.
You just fade out!
Die, O professor!!

My Freezing Heart
(John Donne wrote a poem with this title – 1633)

Must I pile red roses and bandsmen?
Bachelors to sing in unison
About my freezing heart?
Must I hire a professional chest-beater?
A *Noha-Khwan* نوحه خوان as they say in Farsi
To wail aloud, grieve and mourn my loss
And beat his breast for me
Crying a cacophony of
O I die, I faint, I fail?

Is it really becoming?

I was a ripening disaster, I know
Sans-redemption, without retrieval
No conscience pangs did I deserve
For no escape was possible
The calamity was but a foregone conclusion
The cataclysm was of my own making
The portents were known by me.
So why be sorrowful?

Is it indeed befitting?

It took half a century
Indeed, fifty years for the disaster to ripen
Not short and brisk
Nor sprucely in *a la mode* style
But laggardly, dim-wittedly
It kept its dumb ruin gathering momentum
Till finally it reached its apogee

The apex, the *ne plus ultra,* as it were
For the heart to deep-freeze
Stop squirming
And, finally, stop beating altogether.

Befitting it might have been
Years earlier when it was still young
Full of life and its breezes
To tell it that the path it chose
Slow and steady though it was
Was really heading it to destruction?
The poor throbbing machine of muscle
Might have known what was coming
Could I have checked it, stopped in time?
I guess not.

Befitting it might be now at least
To slit open the chest with a gash
And see the poor bastard
As it lies dead and drained
Of life and its loathing for life.

What if it had not chosen that path?
What if?
What if?
Questions galore – no answers do I get.

A Harlem Dancer

(Claude McKay wrote a poem with this title—1922)

Sallying, swaying, gliding
She of the Harlem's hospitable hub
The one who knows the poetry of the foot
Verse of the body brightly black
Bustling busy, impatiently excitable
The Queen of Sheba with her queenly act
Stands right here on the raised dancing floor.

A feathery fluttering bracelet bra
Hiding, chiding, showing, glowing
A pair of sprightly, spirited globes
Brisk and quick, arousing, awakening
Satiny smooth and softly spirited
That all can see
Shadowy cleavage to blackberry nipples.

All can see the lingerie lonesome
A strip, a band, a ribbon-like bar
All can see but no one sees it
The overlay lay-in moves in mind
Peeling and paring the puny piece
A streak, a path, a trail to reveal
Not to the eye but to the fancy.

A pole she climbs with buttocks swaying
Roused are all the front row roosters
Mid-rows all but crane their necks
Back-rows pertly peep and pry.

Pole, no vault, no prance, no jump
The Queen of Sheba with so many Salmons
Trying their wisdom of loins
Erect and aloft without Viagra.

The Bathtub

(Ezra Pound wrote a poem with this title—1913)

With Ezra it was the 'slow cooling'
Of 'chivalrous passions'; with me it is
Fast heating and fast cooling
Both in quick succession.

With Ezra it was a 'much praised'
'but-not-altogether-satisfactory lady',
With me it is adequate and gratifying
Even soaking and drenching bathtub satiety.

To Ezra white porcelain lining was welcome
To me the size of the tub matters
Its shape, trim and fettle are important
Fitness and form are recompense
Fuzzier and denser – better for me.

To Ezra giving out by hot water
Or just going tepid was a cool towel
Draining his manly strength – or whatever he had.
To me it is quick, swift and fleet
Here come, hot and hotter still
There go, cool and cooler, push, phish but no fuss!

A True Maid

(Matthew Prior wrote a poem with this title – 1718)

"No, no; for my virginity,
When I lose that, says Rose, I'll die;
Behind the elms, last night, cried Dick,
Rose, were you not extremely sick?"

Was this the way you wrote a host
Of poems in 1718, O Mat Prior (or Post)?
Fourteen? Fifteen? A child no more, a maiden now
A graceful maiden, with a gentle brow!

A cheek tinged red and a dove-like eye
And all Dicks salute as she passes by
She may, one day, be caught by glare
Maids, like moths, do all but care.

Gravity, they say, is a man's deceit
Vivacity, it's said, is a woman's treat
Breathes there men and women so tough
Who say two sexes are not enough?

Maidservant and modesty – thus appears
She will or won't, the old master swears
Not, but lecherous as he is often and much
And seldom faces the truth as such.

A true maid, thus, is a dying breed
With none of Prior or Howitt or Reed
Singing of her chastity here below
Yet each one trying a sham to show.

The Age Asks Ease*
*John Donne: *The Sun Rising. 1633*

In this hot summer in India
There are no frosty flowers
No cool breath of hailstorm
Nor hoar-frost to see on grass
Yet mushrooms are aplenty.

Beneath this tropic sun
Ice never forms
No lips freeze, no hands shiver.
Growth is luxurious
Aplenty and apace grow men and beasts.
Humans do not trifle long
In the vestibule;
Boys do not remain boys long;
Too early they masturbate
And girls become women
Even before they menstruate.

This girl's parents are dead.
Says the pimp buyer to her keeper aunt
"Skimpy and thin but superbly rounded
Buttocks and breasts
Ten? You said, she was
but looks she twelve or thirteen.
Age is a factor in our trade, you know.
How about five hundred rupees?
Come, take a thousand, no more."

A Browningsque Melody

A 19th century young lover's song that loves but writes adolescent verses

Come my love and live with me
So dear a hope embodied be,

A forest Rome, or on the hill
Calming nature to your will.

Come love, my life, and live will I
Yet two score more I'll serenely lie

Your left side, lass, wrapped in your arm
Strong and silent—composed and calm.

Hours are serene and nights rejoice
Two of us alone by our best choice.

Come lie, my sweet love, and live
A golden age imperative

And silken snares and silver hooks
At last are tossed in magic brooks

Where fisher and fish are mutually caught
And interchangeably are wrought

Till each in truth the other be:
Come, I'll hook you as you net me.

On the bank in fire we'll breathe
Not air nor water, each reprieved

As fit for the scene in love's world laid
By half and half a new whole made.

Delay
(Elizabeth Jennings wrote a poem with this title – 1953)

Songs lie frost-bitten out in the back yard
Sung each verse freshly frolicsome only an eon ago.
Albums have all but left with autumn-stricken leaves
Of a story invisibly written on each face faded
Or a tale told in frescoed *lingua iconic.*
Gray faced flowers still tied up as a bouquet
Lie on the table, left there by a ghostly memory.
A voice sans words, a sound sans sense
Keeps knocking against doors bolted, chairs upright
Chairs don't fall, doors don't open.

The sun yawns, peeps from its comforter fog
Doesn't come inside for the windows are shuttered
So are all eyes and ears of the house that plays dead
Yet it awaits a soft knocking or an earthquake.

What was the delay, pray?
Asks the occasional gust of heavy, hoary hail
Striking against the walls it scatters vermin all around.
Only to be frozen into the earth
A dead body unsavorily earthed in a shallow grave
The past – oh, the past!
Eons ago or the last summer, when was it?

What was the delay, pray?

Leda and the Swan

A New Version
(Yates wrote (not the only) old version with this title back in 1924)

A sudden blow indeed it was
Wings indeed they were, white porcelain
Fluttering, frittering, flapping still
When the girl beneath shrieked aloud –
"Oh! I'm being raped!"
None could come to her succor
For the staggering girl and the male swan
Beyond the reach of ordinary mortals ran.

Yates paints the picture
More in white than in black
With graphic words: 'thighs caressed'
'Breast upon breast'; shows the girl
'Her nape caught' in Zeus's swan bill
And 'her terrified vague fingers' helpless
Against the fornicating supreme god
Trying to push him away from her
'loosening thighs'.

'A shudder in the loins', Yates enjoys the scene
As a lusty onlooker describes lustfully keen
Engendering this 'feathered glory' of Zeus
With the burning roof and the broken wall
And the scene of Agamemnon dead
Dreadfully alone – Oh, William, Oh, Butler, O Yates!

Oh William Butler Yates,
Did you see the hapless girl caught in Zeus's clutches?
As a willing recipient, nay a conspiratorial go-getter
Of an Annunciation of the Greek civilization
The same way as the Annunciation to Mary
Would find Christianity?

A Crazy Jane Poem

(Yates wrote a series presenting Crazy Jane as a Wise dame)

My native village in India
Could boast of one *Jamalo*
A crazy lass of uncertain age
Strong yet looking hollow.

Roam the streets she did
With her pajama string hanging
Inside was what everyone
Remembered as often banging.

Jamalo would pull the string open
No sooner than saw a man coming
Men generally fumed and ranted
Yet stole a glance repelling.

Women she met with dismay
Shrank and shriveled in frame
Withered and seared passed them
Tightening her string in shame.

Jamalo, not unlike Jane
Said this on love intent
"Love has pitched its mansion
In the place of excrement."

Jane's words in Yates's poem
Is what I've given in quote
Like tables in math, all lovers
Must read and learn by rote.

Long Legged Fly

(A Yates poem that 'celebrates' Helen of Troy's abduction by Caesar. The title of his poem, he later wrote, had nothing to do with either Helen or Caesar.)

*

(Like a long legged fly upon the stream
His mind moves upon silence) – says Yates of Caesar.

The mind indeed was moving upon silence
Posing a problem he of all people couldn't solve.
The dame was 'part woman, three parts a child'
Barely twelve years old
And Caesar was – ask Brutus – thirty-plus
If not more, but what matters, matters not to men
Even less to victorious warriors.

(Like a long legged fly upon the stream
Her mind moves upon silence) – says Yates of Helen.

My face, launching a thousand ships?
My face, the cause of burning
The topless towers of Ilium?
My face, indeed, my feet, of course,
If my feet practice a tinker shuffle
On the wooden floor and get scratched,
Do they bleed? No they don't
But bleed I did
Only once
You know where from!

(Like a long legged fly upon the stream
His mind moves upon silence) – says Yates of Caesar.

The Master is in the tent
Poring over a set of maps

And the ships are tethered
The way a pony or a dog is.
If the battle is lost, either way,
Trojan, Trojan, ah!
If, if?
Troy doesn't fall and my ships are sunk?
Heaven will not fall nor civilization lost
I will go in history a great general nonetheless.

(*Like a long legged fly upon the stream*
Her mind moves upon silence) – *says Yates of Helen.*

A girl in puberty thinks of a boy her age
Does a boy look like Adam
Painted on the ceilings in Sistine?
No, he doesn't,
The fly moving on the stream buzzes
And repeats, No, Adam in the painting looks a man
More like Caesar than a boy her age.

"There on that scaffolding reclines
Michael Angelo. So shut the doors
Of the Pope's chapel."

(*His mind, her mind, both in unison*
Like two long legged flies upon the stream move.)

Vitae summa brevis sperm nos vetat incohare longam (Horace)

How does one write an autobiography?
From the very first day he learnt his three R's?
Difficult to answer, but for a measure
I'll take my own example.

I scorned the stuff contemporaries wrote
Sang my own songs as they came epiphany-like
Into a recipient mind like a mother of pearl awaiting
A pearl yet to be formed in its uterus.
Conventional phrases? Pooh! I shunned them all.
Dreams occurred – coherent, incoherent, shapely, and shapeless;
All had a meaning and interpretation.
All could be applied to real life.
Flowers and grass and cloudless sky
Verdurous vibration, somnambulant symphonies
Grew in the wakeful mind
And a sculptor, a painter or a poet I was
Clasped each other by brush and paint and pen
And I created my own awe-inspiring autobiography.
(The first letter I wrote when I learnt my three R(s).

Then it was a purpose set for life
No profane self praise, no lauding, applauding
Magnify, glorify – two words shunned and banned.
Meritorious it was that I wrote
Worthy of self, yet critical, censuring if need be
But true it was to self and the world around me.

How do you begin a self-sustained autobiography?
I asked. A Rousseau? A Don Juan? A Casa Nova?
Trash, I said, an autobiography should begin where it ends.

Back track your steps from old age to youth
Youth to boyhood and then to your early age.
Bring the old man's un-jaundiced eye to see what you were.
How can one foreordain what has yet to happen?
Is predetermined fate that ends in despair or doom
Or the one that is ordinary and yet
Exceeds the ordinariness of life.
That would be my autobiography.
Begin at Z and come back to A
Trace your course from pearl to the mother-of-pearl.

My hand drew back, I often sat still
Then it crawled like a snail on the paper again
It wrote and wrote, with left hand, in a long-hand scrawl
Visualizing what might be, not what has been
No dead sea scrolls but scrolls written now
To be discovered, maybe or not, centuries hence.
The sodium light on the table at night
The sun pouring its rays from morn to eve
I wrote and wrote
My life story as it would unfold in years to come.

Today when I have seen eighty autumns
I say to myself, it is perfect
Like the little pointed breasts of brass
Of goddess Tara Devi statue in the corner of my study
Or of a Nubian goddess on the mantel piece.
Go and breathe your last like a contented man
One who could write a biography of self
Ere he lived his life.

A song in translation
Vergissmeinnicht
Forget me Not (German).

'It's painful to part from a friend in haste
Costs us heavily, a sigh and a tear
Live we do, not die in despair
For years to live is not a waste.

The goner, on your unknown course
May yet be changed, Ah, tarry a bit
Bid not adieu, come by my bosom sit
Put off, you can, I know, the divorce.

Don't break this trance of love, O dear
Fair weather and stormy climes we've had
Happy or gloomy or laughing or sad
Laughter or smile – a giggle or tear.

Felt, we have zephyrs that blow
Across the meadows, cool and soft
Heard we have not seldom but oft
Streams that warble as they flow.

Meeting and parting, two ends of a coin
Self-same minted of a singular metal
Yet worlds apart, depart or settle
No ends meet and no shards join.

Cold is your kiss and colder still
Your silence and tears and the last sigh
Echoing but silent, nor far nor nigh
A sundered voice over dale and hill.

A Chance Encounter

Not an encounter but a conjunction
It was; a 'happen-upon' meeting unforeseen
A park in Milano and rain's showery sheen
Pouring down on sight-seers seen, unseen.

She was but a slip of Chinese stock
And I, a six-footer and generously built
The refuge we took was by chance not guilt
'Neath a willow with ivy on a rock.

The space for one, I wreathed her in arms
Petite her body just melted in kisses
In Italy my chances were all near misses
I thought I was back in India's palms.

A cover it was in blustery weather
'Neath a rock with ivy and a willow
My rain coat both a rug and a pillow
Till the rain stopped, we lay together.

And then it was over, done with, gone
Her man came running, jumping as a frog
Short he was but as a hog he could jog
"Thank you," she said – and I was alone.

Died he has

Died he has and you of his progeny,
Live. Life is good—you think—but loudly you say
He is no more, our Pa and Grandpa
No more, yes. Gone forever he is.
His life was good but no less good
Was his dying; didn't teeter and totter on his feet
Didn't have to be fed or taken to the loo.
Didn't give us trouble in his dying days.

   Storm-winds, keening and repining
Rock the house. He, now in illimitable space,
Might have said, the storm-winds sorrow more for him
More than you do, O his progeny.

   Alone in grief is the dog in the manger
Not baby Christ, but dog – the shaggy brute
That brought the ball in his salivating mouth
Thrown at his command again and again.
Alone in grief are the scurrying feet
Of squirrels who were fed all kinds of nuts
Acorns, of course, but costly almonds too,
Asking them never to eat birdies' eggs
For it was a sin to eat others' babies
Yet to be born.
Alone in grief are the birdies to whom he talked
In morning and evening and daytime too
Feeding them crumbs and telling them
Not to fight and scream and make a din.

No friend, no pal, no crony, no none
Alone and apart he lived withdrawn
From all, aloof and cool and formal
Died he has. No lumpy grief does he expect
O frippery friends and fellow fops
Just be forthright and say
Good God, he's dead, after all!

To John Updike
(In response to his poem belittling M. Anantanaraynan)*

John, suffering unashamedly
Of dysentery, as you are often, doesn't mean that you,
A Caucasian with a twisted tongue, words flowing
From both ends, (you only know *which* and *who)*
Should belittle a poet who grew
With a name that needs some nasal blowing.

What's so difficult, man, to pronounce
A hallowed name that means God, the Limitless One?
Ananta means limitless in Queen's English, my friend
And *Narayanan* is one of His attributes.

Well, author-bitten you are probably
For you call all authors 'a dreadful clan
To be avoided if you can.' But Anantanarayanan
You would like to keep confined to Hindustan.

Picture yourself with the man who's a marvel
He 'as short and tan'; you 'as tall and marmoreal'.
And you say you do now plan
To be his life-long ardent fan.

You'd seat him, you say, on a lush divan
More luscious than one in Zanadu of Kubla Khan
And then practice saying again and again
All the "a"s and "n"s together, crazy or sane.

I know, John, you're fond of names
Wigglesworth and Killpatrick and Hughshumphrey
They enter your poems all and sundry
So be at ease, offense is taken anon
By me or by Mr. Anantanaryanan.

A NOTE ON HOW AND WHEN I WROTE THIS POEM

*John Updike, the renowned American poet, wrote a poem titled *I missed His Book, but I Read His Name* (1963), and using his sleigh of words with a tongue in his cheek to make fun of the Indian novelist's relatively unpronounceable name. The title of Mr. Anantanarayanan's book was *The Silver Pilgrimage*, (Criterion. 1961). I had read John Updike' poem in Norton Anthology of Poetry, a textbook that I used for my undergraduate students. It rankled in my mind for I always had great regards for John Updike. Almost a year junior to me in age, we were contemporaries in more than one sense of the word. The chance to talk to him came pretty late in my life as I got involved in my domestic affairs. However, a few years before his death, (He died on January 27, 2009), I left a message with his secretary that I would like to meet him for a few minutes. He called me on phone and said he would be happy to meet a fellow poet from India. The date, time and place were settled. I had to meet him in the office of *The New Yorker,* and from there, he said we would go for a drink and a bite.

Our meeting was a great success. I found him a jocular person, ever ready to laugh. When I referred to his poem, he said that he had read this unpronounceable name in *The New York Times* and was so given to its nasal twang that he practiced pronouncing it. When he couldn't, he wrote the poem but it was not done to belittle the gentleman whom he had never met. Anyway, I told him that I had written a poem addressed to him. He was intrigued. He told me he had never had anyone write a poem addressed to him. A drink or two later, I read out the poem. He laughed at almost every line of it. When his laughter subsided, he said, "Come on Satyapal, let's have a wager. If you can pronounce the gentleman's name five times without stuttering or stopping, I will give you twenty dollars. If you can't, you will give me fifty." I got the catch. "Don't act the Jew with me, John," I said, "Twenty it is for both of us." He laughed. "All right, let's act Hindu with each other. Twenty it is each way."

It is an interesting story, but the fact of the matter is that I lost the bet. The first two times I succeeded but at the third time I stuttered and lost the momentum to pronounce *Anantanarayanan* in one breath. I would say *Ananta* and then pause for a mini-second before continuing with *Narayanan*. He was happy with himself. He said, "Let me sign your poem so that you have a record that I approved of it." He signed the poem with my pen. I have treasured the piece of paper ever since. Here is his signature on my poem.

The Doomsday Painter

There he stands!
A canvas strung on an easel
Paint brushes held firmly in his fingers
Holding fast to them
Afraid that if his hand loosens up
His brushes would drop in the dust.

There he stands!
His blind eyes riveted on the horizon,
He looks with a squint to see
If there's a message writ, a tell-tale sign
An omen that he might read to help him
Paint his picture of tomorrow.

There he stands!
Oblivious of his surroundings
Colors, dry and liquid, pastels and sticks
Lie scattered all around him.
Maybe, he scattered them in his day-long slumber.
It is evening now and he must paint his picture
Before it is dark for then his blind eyes would shut
No sign, no symbol, no tell-tale omen would be clear.

There he stands!
The paints that are scattered
Colors of death and destruction; they convey
Dark, dirty, and degenerate decay
Rotten and retrograde hues
Like slivers of dead skin
Smallpox boils oozing puss

Worms eating live worms
Defecating dead worms.
Paints, dry and liquid, pastels and sticks,
Grimy, grubby, filthy and foul.

There he stands!
What message is writ, what portent portrayed
That his blind eyes would see and read
Before he paints his picture?
The doomsday painter himself doesn't know.
He waits, just waits for a sign.

There he stands!
Deep inside his crazed self, he knows it all.
When he paints this picture, his fingers would
Imprison the air; it would be a windless vacuum.
There would no 'nadir' and 'Zenith'
No poles of the earth to hold it together.
It would all be over.
All be over.
All be over.
Only God shall remain. Or shall He?

Parrot Palmistry in India

On the highest twigs above
Unmoved
Two Polly seed parrots are talking
Chatter chatter, chitter chitter, the say
What they mean is their keeper's name
Chatterji he is called – and that's his family cognomen.
They are let out of the cage early morning
They chitter chatter their way around
Pluck whatever raw berries they can pluck to eat.

Winter sunshine reddening through
A circle of a keen-eyed eagle spreads overhead
And parrots chatter their way back to the cage.
They open the door with their beaks
And then shut it tight to feel safe.

Parrots are Chatterji's working hands
As they were his father's or his grandfather's.
Come late morning and a feathery day
And he'd take his trade tools to the bazaar.
A shanty town of Calcutta is his workplace.
Two parrots in a cage, a bag of berries
A neatly packed stack of fortune-telling cards
And lastly himself, the master of all ceremonies.

On the back of his own palm
A parrot with a long beak is tattooed
His father had told him he was born that way
But he knows that it was tattooed
By a wayside tattoo-engraver for just one rupee.

Spreads his mat and sits aplomb
A group of youngsters surrounds him
Aimless wanderers, jobless looking for work.
One pays him a coin and he lets one parrot out.
The parrot goes carefully to spread out stack of cards
Chooses one, rejects it, chooses another
Holding it in his hooked beak, he waits for his wages
A berry or two – and then hands it over to him.

He gives the card to the customer to read.
"You are fortune's favorite. You'll get a lottery prize,"
And then adds as a Post Script, "If you're unconvinced
Then feel your backside. You have a big mole there."
The man's hand steals back in his shirt to feel
And then he's happy for he has found a mole there.

Two, three, four, five – customers come and go.
Happy are parrots for the feast of fresh berries.
Happy is Chatterji for he has earned the day's wages.

Monody

A keening rhapsody of the worst kind

Necrology priests don't ever keen
Obituaries they've never seen.
Friars do their paternosters' duty
Rise from th' dead an' collect their booty.
The corpse, a man in his seventies
Had probably lived in livid vanities.
Sideburns—clipped decimal to the point
Moustache—no hair missing for a joint.

One, like many, I was also there
Close by th' sable woman, his heir
How come, said one, a weather-beaten dame
Ebony-like color, could carry his name?
Said a whitely brother of the cast
Black's no bar if a wife's steadfast
Sham might've been with a whitely dame
A colored husband just dying of shame.

Portrait of a Lady
Portrait d' Une Femme
Portræt af en kvinde
Porträt einer Frau
تصویر ایک خاتون کی

There she was, one of the tribe literati
A part of the crowd jamboree
And I was there too, the youngest among them
A scribe with a fresh brown face
Others all grizzled, grizzlies obese
And she, a Venice with arms still in tact
Writing in a flowing hand – fully ambidextrous
With one or the other hand, both industrious.

Mesmerized, I, for once, sat quietly
Watching, just watching her, admiring
Admiring her dexterity of writing with both hands.
Suddenly I recalled a Donne poem
Years ago, in student days I had read.
Why did I recall it, I don't know.
The seminar note book I opened, wrote it verbatim
Tore off the page, got up to go out
Passed her by, placed it in front of her.

A second it took, but up she did look
I hadn't stopped but pushing her chair back
She got up too. Let's go for a cuppa', she said.
With her Lathe and my Espresso, we both sat
And she pushed my hand-written slip in front of me.
"Read it," she said, and again, "Read it, please."

I read—and cherished my reading
Adept I was in reading poetry aloud.

She heard – a picture of Venice (with arms)
It looked she cherished her hearing too.

She's all States, and all Princes, I,
    Nothing else is.
Princes doe but play us; compar'd to this,
All honor's mimique; All wealth alchminie,
    Thou sunne art halfe as happy'as wee,
    In that the world's contracted thus;
Thine age asks ease, and since they duties bee
To warme the world, that's done in warming us.
Shine here to us, and thou art every where;
This bed thy center is, these walls, thy sphere.

It took all my might to open my eyes
For I had read it from memory, with eyes shut.
Watching she was, me? Or something beyond me?
Her blue eyes open wide and wider still was her stare.

"Goot, goot," she said and I knew for certain
She wasn't of the English-speaking world.
"Goot, goot," she said again. *"Thou read'st well."*
And with her snow-white hand covering mine brown
She added, *"No English, none, a lille bit German, Ja."*
And I said, "Ja, Ja, I know, my princess."

Three days it were and we talked, talked and talked
In words and gestures, body language the most
Was the medium, better it was than words mouthed.
Went out for walks, ate and drank and . . .
Slept together. Hardly ever slept.

Come the last day. She was sad
Sadder still I was but I knew it had to be
It was always like this, I knew
And would always be like this, I knew that, too.

Sad she was but on the same table
With her Lathe and my Espresso
She said, "Read me *un* more, please, please."
And Donne, my friend, came handy
I said, "I don't know what the title is
But my title of his poem is *Nirvana of Love*."

I read, *"Now thou has lov'd me one whole day,*
Tomorrow when thou leav'st, what wilt thou say?
Wilt thou then Antedate some new made vow?
     Or say that now
We are not just those persons, which we were?
Or, that oaths made in reverentiall feare
Of Love, and his wrath, any may forsweare?
Or, as true deaths, true maryages untie
So lovers contracts, images of those,
Binde but till sleep, deaths image, them unloose?
     Or, your owne end to Justifie
For having purpos'd change, and falsehood; you
Can have no way for falsehood to be true? . . . .

Cut me short, she just did, and said "No, no more.
I've read this poem before.
It talks of women's deceit and folly
I don't want to listen to it, no more . . ."

Aghast, I looked at her.
Was it God-ordained or woman-devised
She spoke her English perfectly well
With a quaint accent, yes.
French, Danish and German mixed.

✶

William Loves Mary

30621 LOVES 90756

Out upon it, I have lov'd
   Three whole days together;
And am like to love three more,
   If it prove fair weather.
     (John Suckling 1609-1641)

   Courtly love Suckling detested
Others of his age didn't
He of all Donnes, Carews and Herricks
Depicted love as a physical need
No sugar-coating
No gentleman folding his wobbly knees
And asking for a dame's hand.

   Hand? Today's poet might have asked.
Who wants a hand? It's the whole *fe* , a male wants
Not just a hand.

   Quote Suckling again
"If of herself she will not love
Nothing can make her
Devil take her!"

   What Suckling did
The modernist poet does better
To him if Mary has a number and no name,
What he will carve on the tree is not

Bill loves Mary – but
30621 loves 90756, both of
Blood Group B-Positive
And of English Major Course in the college.

War

Poets, I know, have lauded war
Epics and *qaseedahs* have always been written
To praise the national heroes
Who conquered foreign lands
Or were slain in battles defending theirs.

Were there any, I wanted to know
Who branded war as evil?
Could all poets have been so blind and deaf
As not to see men dying, women crying
Babies whimpering – their parents butchered?

My search took me
To Greece, twenty-five centuries back.
Aeschylus was the one who had the vision
Warriors never come back alive; only their ashes come.

> *Those that were sent away, they*
> *Knew, but now they receive back*
> *Not the faces they longed to see*
> *Only a heap of ashes.*

Hither to thither I searched again
And found Jeremiah writing a century or so
Earlier than Aeschylus and others of Greece.

> *For I hear the sound of the trumpet*
> *The alarm of war.*
> *Disaster follows hard on disaster*
> *The whole land is laid waste.*

Suddenly my tents are destroyed,
My curtains in a moment (are pulled apart)
How long must I see the flying flag
And hear the sound of the trumpet?

I rubbed my eyes; I looked from right to left
Again from right and left and my eyes ached.
Why does no one read the message that was
So clearly conveyed, so explicitly explained?
I went to Vadrashang, the poet in India
An eye witness to the Kalinga war, he wrote
This unforgettable account in Sanskrit.

Three bodies lie sprawled
One on top of the other
A hand is cut, a leg severed
A head split into two
A battle axe it might have been
That accomplished the task
It lay next to them
And the slayer too.

A boy I saw, as young as my own
Still alive in part. Yes, the face was alive
The eyes open, saying, "Water . . . water..
Can I have some?" I gave him a mouthful
And saw he couldn't gulp it down
He had deep gash in his neck.

O gods of war
Do you see down from your chariots?
Do you see? Who dies?
Three brothers together, but not the king
A boy alone, but not the king.

Wang Tsan, he was the one who came to me
Lifting both his hands in greeting.
I come from the second century China,
Nineteen hundred years before your time.
Listen to me, O Satyapal Anand.

Leaving the city
One say nothing, for the horror of the surroundings
Blotted out all else; everywhere
The white bones of the dead were
Scattered and on the roads were starving women
Putting the children they could not feed
Into the grass to die.

What do you remember, I ask myself
A Nagasaki? A Hiroshima? The Mylai massacre?
Come, let me show you for refreshing your memory
Picasso's painting of Guernica
Of the first ever bombing of civilian population.
A shriek in wilderness, still echoing—Do you hear it?

Say I to American Poets

Say I (not shout from the housetop)
To American poetasters, versifiers – poets.
Damn you all, friends, for you're just jokers
Soakers of wet words, plain buffoons
Baboons of yesteryears, you chew your words
Peel them off like bananas
Crunch them up like nuts
Then what? You write a poem, a poem, eh?
And think you've done your best.

See, O nitwits, what I write
I use a pen or a phallus but I do write
Write legibly, readable stuff, and so
At one go
I say to all of you, jesters and judges
Don't make on paper any more smudges.
Take out your pen – or whatever you have
And learn from me to write poetry.

The New Race

Who am I? Asks my hidden self
Not one of many that roam about here
Different, yes distinctly different
From these shreds and shavings, dry and sere.

Shreds and shavings, the average lot
Work and play and earn and spend
And live a mockery of life.
I, not they, am the center, the kernel
That makes the race change and bend.

Alone am I? I really don't know
Others like me would there be some
In this or that nation, here or there
Must they come? Yes, they must come!

A race, prodigious, dexterous, apt
Insightful, knowing, learned and wise
Stands in the wings, waiting
About to become the race supreme.
I am but an early herald.

Imps in a Box

Devil-begotten, Satan's bastards
The imps that sit in this shuttered box
Hold sway over my body, thought and action.
The box – a rounded sphere, I carry all the time
On my shoulders; connected it is with my neck
And the trunk below.

My head, the shuttered box, is the imps' heaven
They sit in front of a switch board
Punching, pulling, clicking buttons
All at their own sweet will
No one tells them what to do.
Send urgent messages to the body below
To say this, to do this
Or not to say this and not to do this.
No reasons why these orders can't be obeyed
The limbs are runners, couriers, servants
Ever ready to do their bidding.

How can I ever get rid of them?
Can I really do something? I ask myself.
The answer comes again from the magical box
No, you can't do anything.
We are here to safeguard you.
We are your custodians
O the lower and base part of I.

True, what they say is true.
I can't do anything to thwart their control.
They are all powerful . . . but
Suppose I take a sharp instrument
A machete—

And cut my head off?
Then? Where would they be then?
Pat comes the answer from the top.
We wouldn't let you, man. Try and see.

To Whom It May Concern
I am going to sever my head today, come what may!

Thanksgiving Day

Thanksgiving day? Is it tomorrow?
No school? What kind of thanksgiving it is?
My eight-year old asks a four-in-one question.
And I really don't know what it is all about.
Is thanksgiving day a Memorial Day?
Are we giving thanks to some person?
Some important date? Or some occasion?
Is it a celebration or a day of mourning?

Memory is not the result of conscious processes
My inner-most self tells me in plain prose.
You either remember who you had seduced
Three years ago when you met her on the beech
Or you don't.
Remembrance is different.
Unlike memory, it is mindful.
It's about consciously examining and
Altering your attitude about events of the past.

Veterans' Day . . . We remember our fallen soldiers
And pledge to look after those not killed in wars.
Remembrance Day . . . Both Canada and America
Remember what? I have heard but never paid attention.
Maybe, it is like thanksgiving, for something given to us
And never properly thanked for.

Comes Nietzsche and tells me
"I did this," says my memory.
I cannot have done this," says my pride
My pride always remains inexorable.
Eventually, my memory yields.

Buried Alive

The cemetery scene was indeed colorful
The burial was of an uncle I was friendly with.
I didn't know he had so many mourners.
They came in their Sunday best black suits
Flower bouquets – colors befitting the sad occasion.
There were men – and, of course, there were women
All had known the deceased in his life.

Overheard I did, bits and snatches of talk.

"Great he was, both with wine and women
Wine, his own, but women? Well, mostly others'!"

"True to his kind, he never lent money to others.
Took some loans himself though.
His estate will have to pay now."

"Calculating, careful to the limit, he was."
One of his nieces made a funny comment.
She said, "he has marked each pencil or pen
He is bequeathing to this or that niece or nephew."

"He should be a model to be followed.
Imagine, dying at ninety and leaving no widow!
Married four times, divorced them one after another.
Great, I say, good and great.
He knew how to live his life."

Didn't I tell you I overheard bits and snatches?
Well, one more that I heard was about me and him.
I'm not going to write about it.

A Filthy Relationship

Straw-thin, soot-black, limping, not lame
The man wasn't much to look at
One would glance and turn away in disgust
That's exactly what I did – but, then . . .

The dame made any one look twice
A strange pair, he, the worst specimen of manhood
She, the prettiest female one meets in a whole day.
Curious I was, thanks to my inquiring spirit,
To know the kind of business they were conducting
Standing cheek by jowl, talking in undertones
Next to the escalator that took you down to the metro.

I stopped and furtively took the space behind them
Trying to put a coin in a newspaper vending box.
" . . . Now, don't delay, just go, girlie . . ."
He was saying, holding her by her fair arm.
"You know the house number, don't you?
Taxi would not suit that neighborhood
It is just next to the Wheaton metro.
The oldie would be eagerly waiting.
A hundred is normal, but you can squeeze out more.
See, that you do – of course, for me is fifty.
Over and above that, whatever you can get.
Now, don't delay, go down and catch a train."

Pimp, son-of-a-bitch! I visibly spat.

Miriam and her Babe

The scorching sun of Calcutta in India
Soaked the pavements with rain for a break –
And then burnt the heavy atmosphere again.
A concrete-steel behemoth under construction
Men and women work like ants
Crawling, creeping, on thin legs
With heavy loads on their heads
To and fro the basement, already built
First floor and second floor under construction.
The whistle for mid-day break is sounded
And the workers, one and all, swarm outside.

A woman I see come to the pavement
Where I waited for a passing taxi or a rickshaw.
Thin, clad in just one *dhoti* , she looks at me
Doesn't say anything but gestures for me to move.
A few steps down the street, I stop and look back.
She goes to a sparsely grown tree on the side.
A cotton sheet tied to the crook of the tree
Yields a squirming baby that she takes to her bosom.

It is her break and the feeding time I know.
Sitting cross-legged where I stood a moment ago
She rocks the baby and feeds it at her breast.
I want to take a photograph of the heavenly sight
But she turns her face away in anger.
I fold my camera in its case once again.
The whistle sounds; it is the end of the break.
She takes a while longer to bundle up the baby.

A man comes running and shouting
"Hey, Miriam, put your brat back and come to work."

The only thought that comes to me is
If her name is Miriam really
The baby's name should be Jesus.

Companionship

An unpaved village road in India
A bit sandy, uneven, stone-strewn
Connecting sand and stone, a query and a river.

A male camel yoked to a camel cart
Used for ferrying stone to building sites
Pulling the cart rather slowly, listlessly
The beast of burden taking a fast step or two
Then slowing down and finally stopping.

When the driver hits him with a whip,
The foam flying from his mouth increases
But unmindful of the punishment
He reverts to his slower pace in no time.

There are two riders in the cart.
One is the live driver with his whip.
The other is a dead body —
The body of the female camel
That had been his life-long companion.

He is ferrying it for skinning.

Contrast

A live scene from the sun-room of a nursing home
The old, the elderly, the decrepit – and the lot
Nursed, taken care of, tended in the 'home'
A one-on-one care home, as it is touted,
Are helped by nurses to sit or lie prostrate
In cushioned chairs with mechanical aids.

The worn out human frames show a contrast
With nurses' uniforms, white, crisp and fresh
Human decay and deterioration
Human Senility and dilapidation
Human glow and effervescence
Matched and contrasted.

The Wake Has Begun

Christmas, Christmas, Christmas
Say all the portents, from floor to the ceiling.

Colorful paper trimmings
Bobbed, wooly, hair-fine braces and brackets
Embroidered paper snakeheads
Vividly brilliant streamers
Flowing like rivulets
Walls, windows, windscreens, wide
And narrow, all decked and furbished
Festooned and embellished Barbie dolls
Toys ornamental and mechanical
The room gives a joyous, jovial, jolly look.

A Christmas tree, cheerfully decked
Showy, bright, fine and vivid
In ornamental lights, convivial and buoyant.
Ten or twenty gifts and presents
Wrapped up with professional finesse
In grand, glittering paper
All methodically arranged under the tree.

The dining table replete with food
Loaded with drinks, crammed with cake
Brimming with beauty and bounty.
Ten chairs all around methodically placed
Waiting for ten guests – the whole family.

The wall clock has struck the midnight hour
The Grandpa – alone and lonely, all by himself
Sprawled on the sofa, dozes off awaiting
His family, sons, daughters, children all.

Where's everyone? Ask the chairs
The food and the tree and the decked room.
Where's everyone? The wake has begun!

No one dies of hunger

Says Kafka
Probably with his lone tongue twisted in satire
No one dies of hunger.
Look at Russia's Gogol
Starved for eight days in a shuttered room
Couldn't die of starvation – crept to the wall
And died of striking his head against it
Again and again.

Says Kafka
Even if the hunger artist calls upon death
To come and deliver him
Death stuffs its ears with wool.
Doesn't care to carry a starving man to hell.

Says Kafka again.
Meet it is for the hungry man
To bite the skin off his own arms
Legs, cut his fingers with his teeth
And munch joyfully.
Lick up every drop of blood that flows.
Blood, one's own or another person's
Blood is blood, edible, life-giving.

How can one convince Kafka
In Knut Hamsun's strong language
If a hunger-driven man cannot eat himself
He can go out and eat the obese
Butchers that thrive on human flesh.

The Circle within a Circle

A circle revolves within another circle
It is as yet half-made, desultory, moving aimlessly
It hasn't found its pivotal center
A nucleus it has yet to dwell upon
To move up and above within the axial median.
Movement it has, but unsteady, irregular
Shoots up a little but can't stay up
Every time it has to come down.

How did it create itself within another circle?
It doesn't know how and why of its origin.
Certain it is that nothing from outside helped it.
It was just born from its own core.
Once born, it imitated the master circle
Moved and moved, revolved and revolved
Till it had an existence of its own.
Smaller but sharper, it tries its level best
To reach the rim of the bigger circle.
It might one day, but not at the moment.
Now it is confined in its own peripheral caliber.

The tiny one within a big circle is in a hurry
It wants to grow, to get big, to increase its sphere
Of late it has gathered such speed and velocity
Such quick movement in its revolutions
The bigger circle is afraid of its growing danger
That comes from within its own heart.
A touch is electrical death, instantaneous, it knows.

The inner one at last touches the outer one.
Sparks fly. Such a din is created that both withdraw.
Then it dawns on the healthier, the bigger one
That the rival, born from its very core
Is a cancer cell that lives to eat others.

Still Birth

A quake it was!
The earth tumbled as if hit by a meteorite.
She felt squeezed under the inexorable burden.
Said something inaudibly low in tone
"I've lost my pearl . . . Please
O please, someone help me find it."

The drip in the right arm vein
Helped her a bit; she opened her eyes
The quake had come and gone.
Her pain dissipated like fog
And she felt weak, but rested.
She went into a spell of drugged sleep.

A boat swollen with precious cargo
She swayed on calm blue waters for eons.
Catching hold of herself or something like herself
She floated and wafted, swam and skimmed
With every big and small wave
She sailed, drifted aimlessly
Didn't drown, for her breathing was even.

Feeling soft and baggy, finally she came to.
There was jetsam and flotsam all around.
The wreckage seemed complete, leaving debris only
The bed was soaked with blood
A nurse was pulling the plastic sheet from under her
Floundering, hobbling – she still was sea-sick.
She saw her thighs being cleaned.
The doctor looked at her, said, " . . . I'm really sorry
I couldn't save the baby."

Cried silently, sobbed and sniveled.
Tears flowing down her cheeks
She knew her pearl was lost forever.
Dead, it came out of the mother-of-pearl, her uterus.

My own Urdu poems in translation

R-e-l-a-t-i-o-n-s-h-i-p

This poem was originally written in Urdu under the title (ر ش ت ه *)*

Two ends of a chord invisible
The thumb and the index finger holding each end
The related duo
Unaware of the strength of this relationship
A bound-unbound liaison
Sanguinely bonded, yet weakly related
Dependent entirely upon two little limbs
Extremities of the body – the thumb and the finger
Just two puny ones were to hold a strong bond.

Unfixed and flexible all other limbs
The two tiny ones might jerk and pull
Slip and hold again, loosen up their grip
Suddenly; rein up and redouble the hold
Continue holding the thread
Of mutual rapport without communication
Intimacy without union.

How long, how strong, how week
How tight, how loose – variables, unfixed, germane
Slip, let go an inch or two
Soften and slacken yet a bit, hold tight again.

Accord, discord . . . R . . . and . . . . E
Enjoin, disperse . . . L . . . and . . . A
Combine, divide . . . T . . . and I
Merge and split . . . O . . . and . . . . N

Unite and sever . . . S . . . and . . . . H
Knit and dissect . . . . I . . . and . . . . . P

Relationship is now a hyphenated chain.
R – E – L – A – T – I – O – N – S – H – I – P

How would the evening end?

Originally written in Urdu under the title ختم ہونا شام کا

A punch-drunk stubborn evening it is.

The sightless night-ghouls cry in the distance
Harnessed with a wet rope to the tethers of the sky
The demons of darkness with their wooly tongues
Not unlike black goats to be butchered
Pee their mortal dread constantly in the wet air.
Drop by drop, it drips from awnings and roof gutters.

I know of many such evenings
Punch-drunk and stubborn
Not prepared to merge into night.
I have stood on this balcony
On the twentieth floor of my apartment building
Almost daily, watching the lights dimming
And darkness engulfing the millions of souls that live
A worse-than-death life in this metropolis.

Atlantic trade winds blow . . .
Leaving behind stench of oil and smoke and dead fish
All intertwined in one gale-like breath
The breath that enters my nostrils
And only then I feel that I am in New York.

(2)

It should be morning time in India – the town
Where my past is asleep like a somnambulist
A grave yard of memories my past is. Each time I
visualize
I try to read the grave stones to see which memory
Is buried in what grave . . . Maybe, others who were

Partisans of these memories also read epitaphs.
Here it is, I tell the other self in me
That my childhood and adolescence lie asleep.

It is morning time in that town of India
Where bikes and mo-bikes, three-wheelers and cars
Vie with each other to forge ahead
Local busses ply to and fro
Kids go to their schools like every other day.

It is morning time in that town of India
Where *you* also eke out an existence of sorts.

(3)

I can see that away from the prying eyes
Stuffed under your pillow are all telltale signs
Of your perplexities and predicaments
The unwritten diaries of sleepless nights
Unspoken stories of what you have to bear
At this young age when other girls
Drink life to the lees.

I can see you getting up and getting ready.
I can see the half-burnt dry slice of bread
A sugared cup of tea as your breakfast.
I know you would go to work
Teach eight hours at a stretch in a school.
Come back, tired, broken-spirited but
With a playful smile on your lips for you Ma.
You would enter the house and say,
"Look Mom, I've brought some grapes for you.
Just taste and see if sweet these are."

The flower of your brow is knotted, I can see.
Your rose like cheeks are pale

Your hair is dry; your lips bluish stale.
You look older than your years.

(4)

Atlantic trade winds, heavy with salt and soot
Bring me back to the balcony of the twentieth floor
Where, a black sacrificial goat, I stand.
The punch-drunk ghoul-ridden evening is
Alive with toy cars running on the road below.
Can I live thru it? I don't know.
I can go inside, become punch drunk and sleep
Or stand here and wait for the evening to end.
The balcony is my sacrificial altar I know
The terrace is open; a small step and a big leap
And my release from life's gaol.
Do I want it today? I ask myself.
If not, how's the evening going to end?

The Lion and I
Originally written in Urdu with the title (شیر اور میں)

Ladies and gentlemen of the audience
Today is my last show, you all know, and hence
You have all come in your colorful best
Laughing and joking and promising yourself
You'll have a good time watching
The lion and its trainer, the man
The beast would sever his neck, and the man
Probably already dead after the first crunch
Would roll away lifeless.
You'll then leave a note for your progeny
The last show of the Ring Master placing his head
In the circus lion's open jaw, you watched with glee.

Ladies and gentlemen of the audience
"Some may go and some may come
The show must go on." You must've heard
This maxim before, for it's our motto.
You know that the sole guarantee
Of my safety is that the lion shouldn't shut his jaw
Not try to pull my head
Till the jazz blows its first note – is my role.
The lion and I, two friends of many years,
Have played our roles punctiliously.
Never has there been a miss or mishap
And you all, in your hearts, pray for it, too.
The din of clapping
The laughter and words like 'Bravo!'
'Well-done!', 'Excellent!' have always been
My badge of honor from you.
Today, there would be no clapping
No words of praise, you'll know why in a moment."

"Ladies and gentlemen of the audience,
Tonight when I place my head in the lion's jaw
And shut my eyes tight – for that's the routine
And backstage the musicians would take
The 'Last Dead March' to its zenith – and
Then suddenly stop it right in the middle,
A powerful beam of light will focus the scene.
My trained lion, my dear friend of umpteen years
My own child, as it were
Will forget his oft-repeated act
And suddenly clap his jaw shut, and
My severed head would roll out of his mouth.

The band may or may not play requiem
The introit mass for the final rest of my soul,
But this I know . . .

Ladies and Gentlemen of the audience,
This much I know.
Both, the lion and I, its trainer,
Have only this way out
Of our life-long bondage to the Show
And with each other!"

Horns

This poem was originally written in Urdu under the title سینگ

Something did happen last night,
He thought absent-mindedly. Well, what was it?
Yes, he could penetrate thru the haze in mind
And see, though not so clearly.
It was fog-laden warmth
That enveloped his whole being
Electric-blanket like, he recalled.
Blood coursed thru his veins like a laser bolt
(Scientist he was and quaint similes were his forte)
And then it had crashed – the laser bolt had hit.
Hot lava squirted out and he felt relief.

His mind, divorced from his lower self
From what was happening with the animal in him
Looked wryly, a little amused; and from above
It watched the scene with a guiltless unconcern.

That was the stale story of the last night
And now he was awake. It is daylight . . .
His upper storey tenant, his alter ego tells him,
Your volcano is lying spent, like a dead rat
Your body has consumed itself in its own fire.
Get up and get going now.

What kind of a hangover is this?
He holds his head and presses his temples.
Something did happen, didn't it?

And then, like undigested garbage,
His mind threw it up. He felt nauseated
Got up, went to the sink, but nothing came out

Except a long icicle of *'sputum a la septic'*.
What kind of a phrase was that? Incorrect? Isn't it?
His upper storey tenant asked.

He closed his eyes again.
I know, he told his detractor, I know it all.
I was inebriated, a self that was my non-self
And what I did was not mine but Satan's doing.
Satan, the First amongst . . . .

He couldn't complete the sentence.
The fog dissipated when Satan's name was pronounced
The First amongst . . . . Amongst what?
Angels or Adam's progeny?
It happens, a matter of course thing, he was told
The 'First Amongst' spoke in a nasal tone.
It happens, you see, he said, it happens every day.
No one cares about these little things of life.
A daughter? Well, yes, a daughter! So what?
A virgin? Of course! Doesn't matter at all!

He went to the bathroom for a shave.
Looked at his face, tired and withdrawn.
Suddenly taken aback he was.
A bit of skin on his temples had cracked
Something hard, the tip of an animal horn
Perhaps, was jutting out
Getting minutely visible.

A Blessing is Turned Down

Originally written in Urdu with the title رضینا بالقضا، استو تتھا

Dimly lit was the shrine's interior
The icon of the god had a hallow of light
Turning it into a source of illumination
The broad forehead with its moon sliver
Gave it the unique peculiarity
Of the well-known cachet for heavenly beings.
Couched in a blanket of darkness
I could see the god's eyes as two live coals
Looking at me with amused disdain.
I knew my innards were alight
With my unconquerable ego.

The god snickered, as it were, in derision
"Come, O seeker, what do you want now?
Your bowl is already full to the brim with
All benedictions that men ask for."
With half-open lips I was about to say something
When he spoke again, as if he knew . . .
An egotist that I was, I had come to turn down
His benedictions and thus feed my conceit
To make him feel, not godly but human
Before giving me a benediction.

The icon spoke again
This time almost as a challenge,
"Whatever I could give you,
I've bestowed upon you already.
Yes, if your purpose is to feed your ego,
Go ahead now and reject my benediction . . .
I'll see how you do it.
Go now with my blessings
You'll live a hundred years, happy, healthy and in comfort."

Eons could elapse in one moment
That was the time I took to think about it.
"Yes, O god, the supreme giver of worldly comforts,
I reject your benediction; I don't want it.
Consider it turned down – I say no to your boon."

Coming out of the portals of the shrine
I felt as if the shining slice of moon adorned
Not the god's but my forehead.

A SEA—INSIDE ME

Originally written in Urdu under the title میرے اندر ایک سمندر

Dead is this sea now
Only a short while ago it was alive
Deep blue, its waves played like nymphs
Sometimes when it was stormy
The nymphs turned into she-devils
Struck their heads against the hills
Scattering rock splinters all around.
The sea played this game for centuries
Succeeded, it did, finally to bore into hill
Creating gulches, chasms, fissures and caves.

Dead is the sea now
But when it is full moon tide
it enters and then withdraws
From its old abode of dry land.
On other days, from far and beyond
Men come in boats, tether their skiffs
Enter the caves and see where holy men
Made their abodes, sat and worked
Away from people's prying eyes
And religious persecution
Have communion with their gods
Meditate and write – and write – and write.

They left their parchments, dried goatskins
Pergamina sheets with words, letters and symbols
All, they thought, would survive for generations to come.
These people were strange, Tourist guides say.
Where they died or were buried
No one knows for there're no graves
No skeletons, no ash of cremated bodies.

Where're the parchments? The leather sheets?
The scrolls on which were written the secrets of the past?
Where are these papyruses now?

Inside me?
Really? Indeed? Inside me? A sea inside me?
O God!

Sperm – Just One

Originally written in Urdu with the title کیڑا

He entered as if he knew the way inside
Entered, yes, entered the depths inside his corporeal self.
What's the hurry to go deep inside my own self?
He asked himself. Then he twirled his manly moustache
Adjusted his distinctive hat, with badges and all
Lifted his arm as if he was addressing a crowd
And said to his inner self, "A brave man I am. Go, I shall!"
Who am I? What was my seed?
What was the soil that gave me birth, nurtured me.
I must know once for all.
I must find it myself, with help from none.
Don't check me, O the Messiah of my sick pulse,
O my mind, don't!

The fog dissipated and he could see
Yes, he could see – a strange phenomenon
Millions of tiny germs, swimming in a dirty gutter
Squirming, struggling, pushing others back
Forging ahead, always ahead to some unknown mark.

Wasn't he also a runner in this race?
Yes, he was. Indeed, he was, he knew it for certain.
And he was ahead of them, writhing and wriggling
Twitching and twisting, ahead of all of them, he was.

He could see his destination now.
A wee little opening of soft, squeezable flesh.
He entered it and went promptly to sleep.
The opening just clamped shut as if it was never open.

"Open thine eyes! Be more circumspect, man!
Will you see your whole life while asleep?"

Someone was saying to him.
Maybe, he thought, it was the angel of death.
"What else has been left for me to see?"
He said and closed his eyes again.

(After a spell of nervous breakdown, this poem, word for word as it is, came to the creative mind under the influence of drugs.)

I and the Weeping Willow
Originally written in Urdu with the title ویپنگ ولو اور میں

(1)

Incessantly it is pouring down
Cross-legged I'm sitting under its canopy
Weeping drop-by-drop, the Willow and I
Have always been companions and playmates.

When she was a little sapling
And I was but a kid-ling
Often we'd sit side by side and talked.
When would it rain? She always asked.
Her voice was the same as the winds' swish-swash
I understood its meaning and tone both.
I would then go up in the sky
Pull down a cloud here and a cloud there
stitch them up together as one
And bring them right over her head.
It rained. It rained and the Willow would weep
Drop by drop, drip, drip, drip, drip, drip.
Her weeping was her laughter too!

Today I'm a seventy years old man
And she's a seventy years old tree.
We've met after a sixty years' lapse
She is indeed very happy and so I am.
An umbrella, an awning, a canopy – I call her.
She likes all her names
But the best she likes is the weeping willow.
"Weeeeppppping Willlllllowowow" She pronounces it.

It is raining and I sit hugging her trunk
Laughing, weeping, laughing, weeping
Her bending branches drip and dance, drip and dance.
She's happy both for my company and for the rain.
I, her seventy years old playmate of yesteryears
Tired, spent-up, exhausted beyond measure
Weary and fatigued, can't even laugh
For it gives me a bout of nagging cough.
With all limbs aching, I bend towards her and say:
"Willow, you're the same as in childhood.
Green and fresh, Fresh and green,
While I, your playmate of the same age
In trying to be the first in every race
Hurt my feet and frame I have, fatigued I am
In body and spirit; it aches, my heart
And my head throbs with blood pressure.
My hands tremble when I pick up a thing.
I've lost the ultimate race, my dear Willow!"

Her tears, dropping, a drum beat
Ask me clearly, "Was it essential?
Was it essential, O my playmate
to come first in all races?
You've lost yourself in winning.
Rooted in one place, I've grown
Right in this spot, that you and I know so well.
When it rains, I weep and laugh, laugh and weep.
I have no ambition to come first in any race."

She takes a swish-swashing breath,
And then says again, "Nothing is lost, friend.
If you've come to your native village now,
Come and be my playmate again.
Come, let's both go up in the sky

Catch hold of the wandering clouds
Knit them up in one big canopy
And make them give us rain."

It is raining incessantly
Willow and I are sitting together
With our arms around each other.

(2)

"Weeping and laughing are one and the same,"
Says Willow when I sit next to her in rain.
"Peel off the laughter's layer from your face
And you'll find it weeping
From your cheeks strip off the cover of tears
And you'll see merriment writ beneath
Think of anguish and elation as one.
Let the steel hardness of your heart
Melt down; make it more like wax
Let tears come to your eyes
For tears show both joy and sorrow."

"Willow, my dear pal," I say, almost stupefied.
"Wherefrom have you learnt this wisdom?
I don't see any books that you read
Nor other friends telling you secrets.
And I? I've always thought
Weeping was a sign of weakness.
Only cowards cry, not brave hearts.
Strong I always thought I was
I could never weep, for . . . ."

Willow cuts me short, "O the Brave Heart,
Listen to me. You could never cry
That's reason you never could laugh.

Had you cried your heart out
You would have laughed your heart in."

"Heart in?" I say, "I can't understand it."
"O, you don't! I thought so also.
In the *tree lingua* it means a healthy heart.
Do you know where my heart is?
Oh, I know that you don't know.
Well, it beats in my roots, in my trunk
All over my branches and leaves, it sings a song
A merry song of drip drip drip drip drip drip
The rain-drops' keening-laughing song.

(3)

"Climbing up and above, up and above
Trying to reach the clouds or the sky
Fixing two feathers with glue to your shoulders
Endeavoring to reach the sun
And falling back on the hard earth.
Taking your buildings and towers
To the dauntless heights of sky overhead
Reaching the stars away and beyond
And thus wasting a life-time—nay, many lifetimes,"
Says Willow, "This, my friend, is foolish,
A foppish frippery . . . . ."

Willow pauses and I can hear the drip drop
The laughing-weeping song she's singing.
"Look at the trees, all trees, big and small
They grow up and above and beyond
But their roots go equally deep in the earth.
No one ever measured their roots
Measuring the height has been your task always.
Count the number of feet the roots go in

Find you will—they're much longer than its height.
You told me you worked as an engineer.
Did you ever measure a tree's roots?
No, you didn't, I know it for certain.
No one has ever done it.
They all measure trees' heights not depths . . . ."

    A pause again and Willow listens to her song.
Then suddenly she says, "You know why my branches,
O yes, these branches that you can touch,
Do you know why they bend towards the earth?
Well, we trees grow out of the soil
But we're in love with our mother earth.
We try to touch it again."

    "O Wise Willow, O my *Tathagata*
You are my wisdom-giver Buddha,"
I say, "And I am your first disciple, Anand."

    But the Wise Willow of a Buddha is busy
Moving and twisting and dancing in the rain.

England, a No-land

Originally written in Urdu with the title بھولا بسرا دیس انگلستان۔

England, a land lost in fog
History? The fog is thicker.
Geography? The fog is the thickest.

A used furniture dealer's stall it is.
Men and women are decrypt and doddering
An aging population, they say.
To me, a visitor from the new world
They look like joker-performers in a circus
Making funny faces, weeping-in-laughter
Or laughing and tear shedding – all at once.
With wooden legs and cane woven bodies
They saunter forth or stop but doggedly walk again.
Buildings and houses, indeed all structures
Built in Victorian times, still standing on weak legs
Reminding how a great nation this was.

Trees, some newly planted but others
Particularly in lanes and by-lanes
Stand crooked, bent or about to fall
Gay greenery it is, looking for a partner.
Parks, roads, wayside pubs and eateries
Look and you'll find them looking at you
Choosing, rejecting or picking a night's bed partner.
Roads, those that go winding through London
Moth-eaten, aged whores that roam about
Woolen coats bought in thrift shops
Goods for sale, hawking their own ticketed price.

The long-forgotten one end of London
Oh, the East End London, you mean?
Well, it is no England, just Paki

With its myriad *Allah-o-Akbar* brand
Men, women, merchandise, *hallal* food
All un-English English.

This *villayat* is indeed not the land
On which the sun never set; it is
But a dark basement cluttered with
Rotten old furniture, broken chairs
Fungus-laden sofas, moth-eaten uniforms
Of the Company-*Bahadur* days of the Empire.
Webster spiders, weaving their webs for centuries
Finally caught up in their own webs hang there
Dead, done and done with – but still weaving
Webs of England's past glory.

I hate my name

Originally written in Urdu with the title مجھ کو اپنے نام سے چڑ ہے

Did I choose my own name? So, why
Should I be known by this name now?
I was perhaps a half or a three-fourth person
Even lesser than this proportion I was
When a name was thrust upon me.

Wasn't a full person, not I
Not half vocal I was
To tell my mother, *Mama Mia*, be careful
Whatever name you might label me with
It might prove false later in my life;
What would I do with this tag tied to me?
A name-tag false fixed on my chest
Wouldn't it prove that I am indeed a liar?
An untrue person, sham personified?

Maybe, when I am a little older
A little mature, I might choose for myself
A name that would portray my real person.
My face, my features, my feelings – all
It might show what I am and what I want to be.
Then only will I not be ashamed of a false name.
Satyapal – a custodian of truth, it means.
I really am not that truthful – and to be a custodian?
I dare not claim that status.

I wasn't able to tell her that
But even if I had been vocal enough to say that
Would she have understood it? I doubt, indeed.

I really don't like my name.

Do Miracles Happen Every day?

Originally written in Urdu with the title معجزے اب بھی ہوتے ہیں

Past midnight it is always
The round face of my beloved moon sends
A soothing and cool ray through the open window
Into the interior of my room and the ray insists
I accompany her outside and go for a pleasure jaunt
On the highways of the sky where star clusters
Wait for me – all agog to see a real poet.

An hour before mid-morning it is always
The fragrant cool breeze with spring in its gait
That knocks at my window,
Says almost in a whisper, "Open it a bit
I'll blow inside so you can hold me to your cheeks.
Let me give you a cloak of fragrance
I gathered from all the flowers . . .
Open your window, just a little bit, please."

An hour after the noon siesta
The fast-running rider Sun peeps inside
Haltingly, with care, its sunlight fingers knock
But then finding me asleep it withdraws
Shame-faced as if it was a crime to wake me up
Or even to peep inside my room surreptitiously.

An hour before supper there's a riot outside
All the neighborhood birds
Blue, brown, red, green –
Indeed all dyed in the myriad rainbow colors
Make a din – especially for me.
Shadows of trees walk by my window panes

Peep inside, say 'Good Night, Friend', and melt away.
The fog rolls down, a brown thick blanket of it
And calls in its hoarse voice,
"It's time, man, take your pill."

    Who says this blighted age
Is not the age for miracles?
Admitted in the hospital, bed-bound for months
I see these miracles every day!

The Slough
Originally written in Urdu under the title کینچلی

He lifted his cactus snakehead a little higher
Wriggled with his smooth, purple-lined body
And then cast away his slough.
Looked keenly into the eyes of the woman
Said in voice, both serpentine and human
"That—which was the forbidden fruit
That—which your God had told you not to eat
That—which you have already partaken of
And found that you have not fallen
From his grace or whatever name he gave it.
Now you know that you are nothing
But a bare body, a naked physical frame
No soul or anything else! Right?"

The woman said in a keen voice
"What have I to do now, O wise serpent?"

"Nothing much, O Eve, it's up to you now.
I have done my part. It is now what you have to do.
Indeed your duty it is to tell Adam the truth
The truth apparent that he is also a body
Bare, uncovered and naked. Nothing else.
No soul, no, nothing."

She understood him the way only women can.
Standing tall and pretty in the Eden
Eve smiled a bit – a satisfied satanic smile
And Satan noticed her appreciation
She looked at herself with admiration
Took a step away from Satan

Looked back at him once more and said,
"O Wise Snake, your own slough you could see.
My slough, you know, I couldn't see
But I've also cast it successfully
And found myself having this gem of a body,
Rest assured, with this figure of mine
I should have no difficulty
In making Adam eat the fruit."

Never be afraid of Spiders

Originally written in Urdu with the tile مت ڈرو مکڑیوں سے

Hanging from the ceiling beams
From windows, bars and handles,
Pictures, paintings and memorabilia
Carefully hung or strung on the walls
Look up anywhere in this closed house
And you see webs, filament booby traps
A network – mesh, tangling, hanging, snarling
Prepared to catch hold of you
Imprison you till eternity.

I tell my three-year old grandson
Just don't be afraid, Sonny, the web is there
But the weavers are dead. Look at the spiders,
Caught in their own schematic mesh
They died long ago. All you see is their corpses
Still hanging dry and lifeless.

Dead are the spiders, Honey, I tell him.
None alive; so are the insects, flying, crawling
The pestering pest, flies, mosquitoes and what-not
Caught, snared, tangled and eaten alive.
The house was shuttered for years
Insects die, no food
And the spiders starve . . .

Never be afraid of spiders, honey
They do a good thing for us, the humans.
Yes, he answers, never be afraid of a spider
Even when it bites you and your hand swells
And you feel itchy.
Isn't that so, Grandpa?

Back To Future

Originally written in Urdu under the title سمت کی مستقبل واپس

You, O poets of South-Asia that I love,
Urdu, Hindi, Bengali and all others,
May indeed be right partially when you tell me
You have come so much ahead that you feel
You can write a new Poetics and a new Republic.

You know what you've achieved
In a few decades after your nations got self rule
The imperialist left you on your own – but
Instilled in you a residue of feelings the prompt
Nothing but inferiority when you compare yourself.
No, not yourself, but your poetry and prose
And plays and novels – and all that you write
. . . Yes, compare with what the Westerners write.

Your ardent desire is to be known 'abroad'.
Abroad? Where 'abroad'? Indeed, where?
Europeans and Americans do not call India 'abroad'!
They might say, 'Well, there in India, or there in Pakistan',
But never abroad, for it is *your* vocabulary pest, not theirs.

So, you want recognition abroad?
A Booker Prize, a Canadian Commonwealth Prize
The Orwell Prize or the Waverton Good Read Award?
No, none, nada – you must have your own standards
Apply them for your own awards in your countries.

I do understand that your prizes and awards are –
Shall we say, not credit-worthy?
One getting an award loses literary stature?

Maybe, the giver shares the cash behind the curtain.
Oh, friends, I know all that
I rue all that, but what can you do?

Your race is back to the future
That just can't be. You have to go forward to future.

The poems that follow are in a different mode. These were written around 1964. I was a visiting scholar at British Council Training Course. Something of a novelty that emerged in the five years was this kind of poetry. Short, terse, fleeting – instant, as if were, words and phrases, stylistically made diminutive having no truck with punctuation – that is how many of us wrote poetry. In a short period of two years that I stayed there (where I rented an apartment) I wrote something like a hundred or more poems. Many of these notebooks, diaries, language lab notation cards and even restaurant memos on which these poems were written have been lost now. Some I could find from my old junk. A part of that junk these poems might be, but I must say that I do not disown them, though I have not written in this style for the past four decades.

Satyapal Anand

Bleeding Together

There is something suspicious
   about living
   as intensely as I do.
   People experience me
   as a threat.

It is not sweat, my friend
   it is blood
   the smell of it
   they are afraid of
   no one wants to understand
   that I bleed
   not for myself
   but for them.

Every day is like
   a bleeding knife cut
   jabbed at my heart;
   don't you feel
   the scab under my shirt?

(2)

I suffer for you
   i suffer for the sake
   of every one of you
   to me each human life
   is an open well
   of tears.

Pain is such a
    terrible fire
    in a blind well
    you can't see
    but smell the smoke
    it comes from
    my heart burning
    deep in the well.

(3)

Do you understand
    what it means
    to lie awake
    and hear
    the world's heart beat
    as if it was
    running for its life?

It is just that no one
    feels human life
    as exposed as i do.

Don't you see
    how i transgress
    my own repulsiveness?

(4)

There's no goodness
    without self-hatred
    and self-hatred
    my friend, is cancer
    you carry—and
    you don't die of it.

(5)

Wait and i will show you
    My wounds
    deep and shallow both
    for i think it is
    the bleeding silence
    jabbed inside me
    by the noisy world
    that frightens
    the innocent skin
    of my friends
    i can sit and bleed
    for hours
    without any one
    noticing it.

(6)

Beloved friends – all,
    i suffer for you
    you see the triumph
    of suffering in my eyes
    but you don't understand
    the reason behind it
    if life loves any one
    it uses the language of pain
    it is in suffering
    that life understands itself.

(7)

Pain, dear friends
    is *a priori*
    for special reasons
    we've known it in this form.

If your strategy
    is gratification at any price
    then you have not escaped
    for with every coital spasm
    as it were
    you're again and again
    impaled on a crucifix.
    understand, my friend
    pain is the ring master
    and pleasure the tiger
    but when the whip cracks
    they are one and the same.

(8)

Pain and pleasure
    our two common
    denominators they are
    two sides of the coin
    you use for the payment
    of a coital spasm
    or a slap on your face.

(9)

Dear friend or foe
    dare not call you a foe
    for you are not one.
    don't you have any
    wounds to show me?
    how wonderful to exchange
    wounds with each other.
    Don't be afraid, my friend
    i like you
    for you suffer like me

i want you to touch
and feel my sore spots
you may call it
conceitedness or fraud
or both
but what i demand is
respect for suffering.

(10)

Suffering is a language
that speaks with
the tongue of love.

Oh, i think
you and i
just the two of us
can sit together
and bleed for hours
without anyone noticing it.

Zero to Zero

Human history ascends
    in circles
    like an aero

Circles vary in color
    black, somber, golden
    pink or bloody red, but
    all alike are divided
    into 360 degree angle.

Counting from zero
    We have 10 angle
    then 20 angle
    then 200 angle
    then 360 angle
    and we are again at zero.

We have returned
    to zero, yes
    but this zero
    is new, a brand new 0
    a different entity altogether.

We went from zero
    to the right
    we returned to the zero
    from the left.
    didn't we?

Human history ascends
    in circles
    from feudalism

to capitalism
to communism
to commercialism
to zero.

Another circle
and it comes back
to zero but a different one.

A Finger Walking

Properly speaking
    i present an unnatural sight
    imagine a finger
    lopped off a hand
    a human finger
    all hunched up and
    bent over
    hopping and dashing
    over the brick sidewalk
    all by itself
    alone.

Believe it or not
    i am that finger
    alone but not lonely
    complete in itself
    biologically
    physically
    and emotionally
    not an entity
    but a totality.

The finger has no desire
    whatsoever
    to be on the hand
    to be a sibling
    of other fingers
    five other fingers
    yes, indeed five.

It is the sixth
    A *chhingli* it is called
    in my mother tongue

the sixth one
the superfluous
the redundant, pleonastic.

It wants to be the way
    it is – all by itself—alone
    for it is I myself
    cut off from all others
    alone but not lonely.

The Drink of Eternity

An ethereal beauty
    a *saqi,* the cup bearer
    golden tresses
    satiny, soft
    velvety, bosky
    redolent of meadow grasses.

She holds a chalice
    sitting on a cushiony sofa
    hugging the chalice
    two mangoes dipping
    into the chalice
    nipples just touching
    as if tasting the wine.

Red lips – cherry red
    drinks a little
    holds out the chalice
    bids me to drink.

Closing my eyes
    i drink
    sweet prickly cold
    sparkles foam and froth
    i drink, drink again.

My blood and
    the universe
    race a million time faster

the earth – a ball
thrown by the *saqi*
flies like a bird.

All things are to me
Light, simple, clear.

A Normal Man

Have you ever met
    a normal man?
    someone usual
    average and general?
    i never have.

The normal man
    is just not there
    a figment of fancy
    a dream personified
    a chimera – in human frame.

From *jojo*, the cave man
    down to the final
    apex of civilization
    namely 'i'
    singular, wayward
    egoist coons
    all are.

Once you catch them
    with masks off
    and teeth bared.
    you'll see
    their ego blazoning
    on their coat collar

Physical Pain

I was transpierced
    twisted into a knot
    by a lightning bolt
    discharge of high voltage.

In our row
    the same row in the theater
    only two seats away
    she came to a stop
    and bent over
    read the number
    and sat down.

A young man
    black Eurasian, pock-marked
    repellently fat lips
    smirking
    sitting in the next seat
    had kept the seat
    unoccupied for her.

My first thought was
    why are you with him?
    why didn't you want me
    to consort you?

I didn't rush over
    i didn't shout
    i didn't even sigh

An invisible spider web
cocooned me
hand and foot, immovable
gritting my teeth
i just sat slouched.

If there can be
in the nature of things
physical pain
from a non-physical cause
this was it.

Rancid Ectoplasm

I am a ghost
    i want
    what every ghost wants
    a host body
    a female host body.

After a long time
    moving thru odorless
    colorless alleys of space
    where no life is
    only grey convolutions
    of gristle laced with soot
    time feces and black blood
    filters of fleshy desire
    I am in the mood
    for love.

A demon lover
    who would want me?
    mine is a yen
    of mindless craving
    a need without feeling
    an earth-bound ghost need
    of rancid ectoplasm
    the opiate of female funneling
    of a ghost without a body.

Once it's over
   the vampire must act
   like a gorged boa-constrictor
   a dietary artist
   to coil and repose—and
   go to sleep.

Man, Machine and Fantasy

every spark of a dynamo
    is a spark of pure reason
    every thrust of a piston
    is an immaculate syllogism

the philosophy of atom
    of electron and neutron
    is as finished and clear
    as a circle drawn
    with a pair of compasses
    or a sonnet by Shakespeare

the beauty of mechanism
    lies in that which
    is undeviating and exact
    as in pendulum
    as in rhythm
    hence poetry & geometry
    consider are twins
    cut asunder at birth

is our schooling for life
    we who have been nurtured
    on logic from our childhood
    have we not become as exact
    as pendulums
    or as theorems of geometry

there ! wait a minute
    I tell myself
    mechanism have no fantasy
    we have

did you ever see
    a wool gathering
    senselessly dreamy smile
    spread over
    a computer's face
    while it is showing its monitor
    and clicking its logic away

did you ever hear
    any robots tossing
    restlessly in bed and
    sighing of nights
    you never did

fantasy is a worm
    whose boring inside
    inside your mind
    leaves black furrows
    on your brows

fantasy is a fever
    a fever that gives you
    on to further flight
    even though the last point
    may begin
    where happiness ends

let us conclude
    fantasy is the last barricade
    on the road to happiness.
    happiness is computer precision
    happiness is geometrical exactitude
    happiness is robotic accuracy
    happiness is . . .

The Horned Beetle

turbidly, dully
    the bluntly speckled head
    of the beetle shows in an
    aperture of the leafy lot
    left by the gardener

hideous the insect is
    yellow eyes seem to keep
    persistently repeating
    the same unvarying thought
    incomprehensible to me
    but a thought nonetheless

for a long time
    we look into each other's eyes
    the yellow shafts from insect eyes
    penetrating the depths of my being
    disconcerting it is
    terrifying also – a bit

what if the yellow-eyed
    creature, i think
    living its uncalculated life
    among its ridiculous
    heap of leaves
    is happier than me

bastard son of a bitch
    (wrong – i should've said a beetle)
    lucky son of a bitch
    i repeat and lift my hand
    the yellow eyes blink
    back away and disappear
    into the leafage
    and leave me to my misery.

Night and I
Dedicated to Urdu poet Majaz Lakhnawi

night it is
>   a white night
>   neon-bathed gas-swathed
>   greenish glassy ghoulish
>   city
>   newyork
>   under a thin glass shell
>   of reflected light
>   everything swirling
>   rushing humming throbbing
>   buildings and cars
>   metro and buses
>   farting
>   billows of smoke

moon it is
>   elderly tired street walker
>   smiling kinkily
>   what does she want
>   me? No!

stars are
>   sprinkled dust-specks
>   snatch them
>   shall I
>   out of the sky

a strange sensation
    my ribs are iron rods
    and my heart
    cramped in their strait-jacket

drunk i am but
    dying, am I?
    it's cold
    i can't do a thing
    except describe the night

Kansa, the Demon King

i am a bad king
  he said
  i kill all first-borns
  before they're born
  or after
  it doesn't matter at all
  it matters a lot for me
  if they grow up
  for all first-borns
  are angels of my death

i turn cities of gold
  into salt
  sandy and gritty
  granular powdery
  sometimes erinaceous
  salty nonetheless
  cities crumble
  minarets collapse
  churches perish
  courts cave in

do you know who i am
  well if you don't
  check your books
  on indian mythology
  i am kansa
  the demon king

why do i do it
    i know
    i am ordained to die
    at the hands of
    a first-born
    so no first-born lives
    in my kingdom.

Facing the Mirror

facing the mirror
    whom do i see
    myself—mine own self
    clearly
    distinctively

whom do i see
    not i
    but someone else's i
    there he is
    this i
    black eyebrows
    straight as if
    they were
    drawn with a ruler
    and between them
    a scar
    a vertical wrinkle
    steely grey eyes
    ringed with shadows
    steel rimmed glasses
    behind the steel
    and the glass
    a soul-less chaos

NO. with a period.
    it is not the 'i' that i know
    it is someone else's 'i'
    does the mirror
    tell a lie?

Lilies-of-the-Valley

well, here they are, i said
    your lilies-of-the-valley
    right here, look

here, take a sniff
    they've a lovely smell
    o, they do
    sniff and test
    your sense of smell

lilies-of-the-valley
    do have a lovely smell
    granted that
    but then a smell is
    but a smell
    lovely or ugly
    you don't look at it

here's the smell of
    lilies-of-the-valley
    and there's the abominable
    smell of hen-bane
    both are smells
    you wouldn't like the henbane

lilies-of-the-valley
    of course
    but they grow
    where hen-bane

also grows
the poisonous nightshade
look at it
but never smell it
stick to lilies-of-the-valley

Postscript

Rummaging through old records, diaries, note books, class-room jottings in search of my long-lost poems may not be like trying to find the proverbial needle in the proverbial haystack, but it is indeed a time-consuming task and it took well nigh six months in finding these compositions. I have pinned a kind of tag to the chest of each poem saying if it was originally written in Urdu or any other language that I write in. This might give an idea of how much of a brain-clutter I am. I write too much, at too many times, with too many *genres* of literature, in too many languages – and I have followed this anarchic mode of working for six decades or more. A poor organizer that I am, things remain scattered in the three bedroom condo I live in all by myself. Sometimes when I look for one thing, interestingly I find a dozen that I had searched for everywhere but couldn't find.

These poems, mostly written in English, but some in Urdu or Hindi are now wearing their American dress. Sartorially a traditionalist that I am, some of these poems will be seen wearing Victorian or Georgian dress in England of the last century, some in today's traditional dresses in India, and some in washed-out jeans and undershirts, Latino style in U.S.A. I offer my apologies for all this poppycock and rigmarole. For those who can discern and for those who know me primarily as an Urdu poet, I have just one comment – a clarification
without an apology. The poems composed in English have a different tone, tenor and style while those trans-created from Urdu into English look like some kind of an imposition on the English idiom as we know it. I have tried to overcome this difficulty, but *trans* is *trans,* in language as in any other field; it cannot be *originalis.*

I am, however, satisfied that what I have done is in the best interest of the stultified American poetry that I read every day – in my classroom where I teach courses in contemporary American poetry—and, of course, in the best interest of my own poetry that comes to shake hands with it almost as an alien being from another planet.

I must add a word of thanks for three friends of mine who have helped me in digging out some of the 'lost tribes' of my poems that I didn't even remember I had written. These friends are A. Abdullah and Amjad Husain both from U.S.A., and Sadaf Mirza from Copenhagen, Denmark.

Satyapal Anand
31 December 2011